DO NOT REMOVE
CARDS FROM POCKET

ALLEN COUNTY PUBLIC LIBRARY
FORT WAYNE, INDIANA 46802

You may return this book to any agency, branch,

or bookmobile of the Allen County Public Library.

DEMCO

SHARKS!

True Stories and Legends

Catherine Gourley

THE MILLBROOK PRESS   BROOKFIELD, CONNECTICUT

SHARKS!

Selection from *The Old Man and The Sea* by Ernest Hemingway excerpted with permission of Scribner, a division of Simon & Schuster, from *The Old Man and the Sea* by Ernest Hemingway copyright 1952 by Ernest Hemingway. Copyright renewed © 1980 by Mary Hemingway.

Selection from *Kon-Tiki* by Thor Heyerdahl copyright 1950 by Thor Heyerdahl reprinted by permission of the author.

Selection from *Blue Meridian* reprinted by permission of Donadio & Ashworth, Inc. Copyright 1971 by Peter Matthiessen.

Photos courtesy of Mo Yung Productions: pp. 3 (© 1995 Norbert Wu), 7 (© 1993 Marjorie Bank), 18-19 (© 1994 Peter Howorth), 24 (© 1994 Brandon Cole), 42 (© 1995 Norbert Wu); Department of Library Services, American Museum of Natural History: p. 10 (transparency #2425); Pacific Stock: pp. 14 (© Ed Robinson), 34 (© B. Brent Black), 76 (© Dave Fleetham); © Ron & Valerie Taylor/Australasian Nature Transparencies: p. 37; John Hamilton Collection, U.S. Naval Historical Center: p. 48; © James D. Watt/Animals, Animals: p. 56; Images Unlimited: pp. 60-61 (© Charles Nicklin), 68 (© Al Giddings); © Board of Trustees, National Gallery of Art, Washington, Ferdinand Lammot Belin Fund: p. 64; © Kelvin Aitken/Peter Arnold, Inc.: p. 84; © Henri Bource, Melbourne: p. 90.

Library of Congress Cataloging-in-Publication Data
Gourley, Catherine, 1950–
Sharks! true stories and legends / by Catherine Gourley.
p.   cm.
Summary: A collection of facts and stories, both historical and traditional, about sharks, their behavior, and their interaction with people.
ISBN 0-7613-0001-5 (lib. bdg.)
1. Sharks—Juvenile literature. 2. Shark attacks—Juvenile literature. 3. Sharks—Oceania—Folklore—Juvenile literature. 4. Shark fishing—Juvenile literature. [1. Sharks.] I. Title.
QL638.9.G66   1996
597'.31—dc2095   45005   CIP   AC

Published by The Millbrook Press, Inc.
2 Old New Milford Road, Brookfield, Connecticut 06804

Contents

To
Jo Gourley,
whose memory of the "green lady in the gulch"
triggered an interest in Hawaiian myths and legends,
and
Theodore Gourley, Lt. Col. (ret.) USAF,
who has always appreciated a story well told.

In gathering the stories for this book, I interviewed a number of talented and interesting people. The only thing they asked of me in return for their stories was that I be fair to the sharks. I hope I have been.

Many thanks to Dr. Robert Purdy of the Smithsonian Institution for his feedback on ancient sharks and his review of early versions of "The Head Hunters." My appreciation goes also to Wes Pratt of the National Marine Fisheries Service in Rhode Island; Charlie Donilon for sharing his great white story with me; Klaus Westphal, Curator of the Geology Museum at the University of Wisconsin-Madison, who first got me excited about mosasaurs; Joe Skulan and Craig Pfeister for patiently piecing together the details of their fossil discoveries in the chalkbeds of northwestern Kansas; Patrice Belcher, librarian at the Bishop Museum in Honolulu, for putting her finger on just the right information I needed; Ken Goldman and Peter Pyle for their insights into the predatory behavior of great whites of the Farallon Islands; and Paul Atkins and Grace Niska Atkins of Hawaii for sharing their unique perspective on sharks in the wild. Finally, a special thanks to Dr. H. David Baldridge, Capt. (Ret.) USN.

PART I
THE ANCIENT
SHARKS

Chapter One
The Headhunters

Sharks are older than humans, older than dinosaurs, older than birds, older even than some mountains. For more than 400 million years, sharks and their ancestors have swum in the oceans and in some freshwater rivers and lakes on Earth. They were swimming and hunting when warm, shallow seas covered most of the land. They were still swimming and hunting when glaciers locked the planet in ice. Sharks are survivors. But how did they survive when so many other prehistoric animals—like mosasaurs—did not? In the true narrative that follows, two young scientists are hunting for an answer.

THE
MOSASAUR
MYSTERY

*t*he Jim Taylor ranch in northwestern Kansas is flat, with dry streambeds and few trees. The nearest town is 20 miles (32 kilometers) away. In winter, the wind wails across the frozen land. In summer, thunderstorms descend like a black curtain, often with little warning. The pounding rain floods the dry streambeds and carves gullies and ravines in the chalky bedrock that is the backbone of the land.

The land was not always as it appears today. Eighty million years ago, a warm, shallow sea spread from the Gulf of Mexico north to the Arctic Ocean. The soft muck at the bottom of the sea became a burial ground for all sorts of marine life—sponges and sea fans, clams and ammonites (animals whose coiled shells could grow as large as tractor tires), jellyfish, and sea turtles. When the sea evaporated, traces of the marine life that had once teemed within it remained—as fossils.

Fossils were why Joe Skulan and Craig Pfeister had come to the Jim Taylor ranch in March of 1988. They were college students and interested in dinosaurs. They wanted to make a great fossil find. Each morning, they woke at six and drove from the ranch to the chalk beds, where the exposed bedrock was the color of cream-of-chicken soup. In the truck were picks and shovels. But before they could dig, they had to discover. And so they hunted in the ravines and washed-out gullies. They didn't know what they would find, but they knew what to look for—shapes. A flat disk similar to a tarnished silver dollar might be an ancient shark vertebra. A smooth crescent could be the remains of a giant sea turtle's shell.

On the third day out, Joe got lucky. A chunk of chalk had recently broken off the hillside, revealing a fossilized bone. As Joe gently dug

9

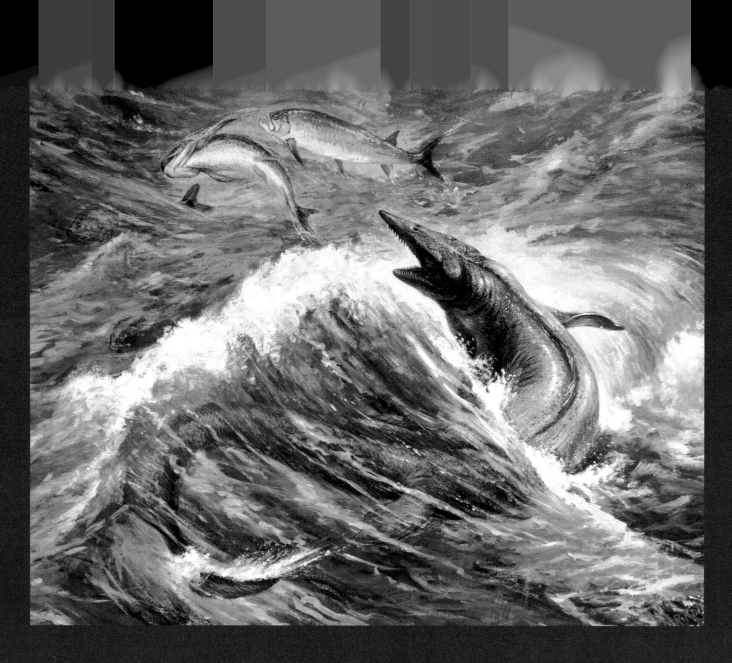

MOSASAUR TYLOSAURUS **BY CHARLES R. KNIGHT**

away more of the soil, his excitement grew. He had discovered—almost by accident—part of an ancient mosasaur tail. A mosasaur was a sea reptile. Its giant flippers and flat tail, 10 feet (3 meters) long or longer, swiftly propelled it through the water like a sea serpent. Like a snake it, too, could unhinge its jaw to scoop up schools of prehistoric fish. With its blunt snout, it rammed and stunned larger prey—tarponlike fish weighing more than 600 pounds (270 kilograms). Its needle-sharp teeth could shatter the thick shells of ammonites. The mosasaur even had teeth in the roof of its mouth.

Forget the dinosaurs! Mosasaurs were the "terrible lizards" of the Cretaceous period. And Joe Skulan had found one, or at least part of one. But it would take weeks of hard work to excavate the skeleton, and Joe and Craig didn't have that much time. Their spring break was nearly over, and they were expected back at school in Wisconsin. Besides, excavating the mosasaur was too big, too delicate, and too important a job for Joe and Craig to do alone. Reluctantly, the students buried the fossil again.

*t*hat summer, Joe and Craig returned to the Jim Taylor ranch with a crew of students and scientists from the University of Wisconsin. They found the fossil just as Joe and Craig had left it. The harsh storms and flash floods of spring had not disturbed it. The team began to work. Under the hot Kansas sun, they swung heavy picks to break away tons of bedrock to expose more of the skeleton. Then, on their knees deep in the ravine, they used tiny dental picks to chip away smaller bits of rock from the fragile bones. Slowly, they tunneled into the hillside and 80 million years back in time.

First they exposed the lizard's tail. The bone had been badly chewed. Next, they exposed the lizard's ribs, then the bony digits of its flippers. The giant fingers were 2 feet (60 centimeters) long. Joe and Craig exposed the shoulder girdle and the vertebrae in the lizard's long neck. Then, 12 feet (3.7 centimeters) down and 12 feet in, they made a grisly discovery: The head was missing.

Had the wind and rain washed away the giant jaw and skull? Joe Skulan didn't think so. After all, he reasoned, the mosasaur had been buried under 75 tons of rock. Perhaps the skull had simply rolled away millions of years ago in the sea currents. But that was unlikely, too. In some places in Kansas, the chalky bedrock is 500 feet (150 meters) thick. The chalk could not have settled so thickly on the sea bottom if strong currents were constantly stirring it up. Besides, the skull was heavier than the finer bones of the flippers. Why would the skull roll away but the flippers stay in place?

There was only one logical explanation. The lizard's head had been eaten by a prehistoric predator. And the only other creatures in that ancient sea who were faster and more deadly than the mosasaurs were the headhunters—the sharks.

Present-day sharks are both predators and scavengers. A predator hunts and kills its food. Did ancient sharks hunt in the same way? A scavenger feeds on dead animals or decaying matter. Was the mosasaur already dead when a shark happened by and stole the skull for a meal? Bite marks on the mosasaur's tail and pelvic bones suggested that the shark might have ambushed the lizard from behind.

Either way, whether it was a scavenger or predator, the shark had had a meal.

*t*wo years after the discovery of the mosasaur, Joe and Craig returned to Kansas and found another piece of the puzzle. Again it was Joe who first spied the fossil in the clay soil, a disk-shaped object that was part of an ancient shark vertebrae. Once again the slow, careful digging began. Day after day, a new team worked to uncover the remains of what turned out to be another remarkable find—a 14-foot (4-meter) ancient shark called *Squalocorax*. In its stomach were the fossilized remains of a sea turtle and some bony fish. More important, its fossilized teeth matched the bite marks in the mosasaur's tail.

Joe and Craig had accomplished what they had set out to do two years earlier. They had made their great fossil find.

Instinct is its mother, too. It watches *Archelon* enter the water. The sea turtle uses her flippers like wings and begins her flight to deeper water. But the mosasaur is faster. Its thick tail whips it swiftly forward. It snags *Archelon's* right hind flipper. The turtle struggles, but does not fight. Her only hope is to flee. With a snap of its jaws, the mosasaur tears off the flipper and swallows it whole.

The splash and the underwater sounds of the struggle alert another predator. *Squalocorax* swims up from the chalky bottom. The shark strikes from behind. It punctures the mosasaur's tail, but just as quickly releases it, then swims back into the cloudy darkness near the sea bottom. The shark has not given up. It is cautious, waiting. The mosasaur is wounded and bleeding. Now *Squalocorax* attacks a second time. Its pointed teeth sink deep into the juvenile's pelvic bone. Then once again the shark recedes.

Soon it will end. *Squalocorax* is both predator and scavenger. When the mosasaur dies, the shark will feed.

Archelon has survived, this time. Instinct tells her to swim deeper, farther to sea, though her wound makes it more difficult. Perhaps already her memory of laying eggs on the shore is dull. Whatever happened to her there in the tropical moonlight is over now. Whatever she has left behind must fend for itself. *Archelon* dives and swims into the milky darkness.

PART II
THE SACRED SHARKS

Chapter Three
The Survivor

In Hawaiian mythology, 'aumakua are powerful spirits, half god and half human. *'Aumakua* can take many forms—spiders, mudhens, eels, worms, and of course, sharks. A shark *'aumakua* serves the person who is its keeper. To strengthen the *'aumakua's* power, the keeper makes offerings of prayers, food, and an intoxicating drink called *awa,* made from a plant that grows on the islands. The story that follows is based on a legend told to generation after generation of island descendants about Pu'uloa, Hawaii's Pearl Harbor. According to the legend, the ancient people of Pu'uloa staged daring underwater duels—one man against one shark. It was a fight to the death. The duels might have honored the shark queen, a powerful *'aumakua* whom the people believed protected their lagoon from the evil, man-eating sharks. The details of the duel are based on artifacts on display in museums—in particular, a wooden dagger with a single shark's tooth lashed to the end. This dagger was the warrior's only weapon as he entered the underwater arena.

In 1902, long before Hawaii became a state, the United States government began building a naval base on an inlet of the island Oahu. Here was a deep and beautiful blue lagoon protected from the sea by a sandbar and a coral reef. The native Hawaiians called the place Pu'uloa. The Americans would later call it Pearl Harbor. To build the naval base, the government dredged a channel from the sea through the sandbar and the coral reef. The dredging uncovered the remnants of what appeared to be an underwater arena built with large lava rocks.

Many native people viewed the construction of the dry dock in the lagoon and the removal of the old rocks with superstitious fear. They believed that Pu'uloa was a sacred place. But the United States government didn't believe in shark superstitions or Hawaiian 'aumakua. Construction on the naval base continued.

Soon after the base was completed, a strange thing occurred. Earthquakelike tremors along the lagoon's ocean floor caused the dry dock to crack and collapse into the water. In time, a floating dock replaced the wreckage. But to this day, the tremors continue. Engineers blame nature and the shifting earth deep beneath the ocean floor. The Hawaiians who still remember the legend of the ancient shark duels have a different explanation. "Queen shark is huhu—angry—and humps her back," they say. "And Smiting Tail slaps his tail upon the water."

On the island of Oahu, a little red-headed girl and her brother had wandered away from their family. The frantic parents searched the island, but the children had simply disappeared! A kahuna, or shark priest, comforted the parents by telling them that their children had been transformed into sharks and now lived in the waters of the beautiful lagoon called Pu'uloa.

Ka'ahupahua, as the red-headed girl was called, and her brother Smiting Tail did not forget their human family. One day, a child was snatched underwater by an evil shark. No one could save her. Ka'ahupahua angrily vowed that never again would evil sharks attack humans at Pu'uloa. From that day on, the people of the island brought offerings to the shark queen. They fed her slaughtered pig and awa. They scraped the barnacles off her back and off the back of Smiting Tail.

To honor their shark queen, the people held great contests—one man against one shark in a battle to the death. At the mouth of the lagoon, the people baited the evil sharks. They dumped meat and fish and other carrion into the water, and then they waited. In time, a shark would come to feed. The people waited until the hungry shark entered the lagoon. Then they quickly sealed off the passage to the open sea with large lava rocks. A sandbar and coral reef formed the sides of the underwater arena. The shark was trapped!

Days passed before the contest began. The shark grew hungry as it endlessly circled the pen. Who knew what thoughts went through the chosen warrior's mind as he, too, waited.

At last, it was the day of the duel. The villagers gathered along the shores of the pen. The shark circled and circled, unable to rest, unable to find a way back out to sea. Then the warrior stepped into the pool. In his hand was a single weapon, a stick on the end of which was lashed a shark's tooth. It was his only defense. He could not run or outswim the swift shark. He had to allow the shark to attack him.

Did the shark charge at once? Perhaps not, for sharks are cautious hunters. Most likely it circled and circled and, with each pass, swam closer and closer to the man standing now waist-deep in the water. The shark circled once more, and the warrior crouched, holding the dagger at his knees so that the shark tooth protruded from between his clenched fingers. Suddenly, the shark shot swiftly upward. The man tensed, allowing the shark to charge. At the last moment, the fish veered away and disappeared into the darker, deeper water again.

And then, its mind now made up, the shark charged again. And again, the warrior tensed. Timing was everything. If he hesitated, the shark would strike a stunning blow, perhaps knocking him unconscious or sending him right out of the water. If he turned too soon, the shark would also pivot and strike.

The shark propelled itself toward the man. At the last moment, the warrior darted out of the line of attack, then thrust his knife up into the shark's soft belly. The fish could not stop its charge as the razor-sharp tooth ripped open its stomach.

This time, the man was the victor and the shark was the sacrifice to the powerful 'aumakua that protects Pu'uloa.

23

OCEANIC WHITETIP SHARK

Chapter Four
A Taste of Flesh

Myths give meaning to life. Some stories of gods and their powers may explain acts of nature, like the tremors that rock Pearl Harbor. Myths and legends can also teach lessons of right and wrong and the power of *kapu*, or things that are forbidden. Perhaps this was the purpose of the story of Nanaue, the shark-man. It is one of the most popular shark stories in Hawaiian mythology. Although the versions vary, the basic story is as follows.

NANAUE WAS DIFFERENT from the other boys on the Big Island. Long ago, his father had gone away and never returned. The boy lived with his mother, Kalei, and his proud old grandfather. But this alone did not make Nanaue different. It was the birthmark on the boy's back. Nanaue had never seen the mark between his shoulders, and his mother forbade him to remove his kapa, or cloak made of woven bark, so that no one else could see it, either. And so Nanaue kept to himself. He did not join in the games the other children played, nor did he bathe with them in the island pools.

As Nanaue grew tall and strong, the birthmark deepened in color and spread. One day while bathing alone in a pool near the river, Nanaue twisted his body until he could see his back reflected on the water's surface. The birthmark had taken the shape of the jaws of a shark. Nanaue knew then who his father was—Kamohoali'i, the shark god.

Kalei was watching from the riverbank. The time had come to tell her son the truth about his father. When she was younger, she now told Nanaue, she had a great fondness for 'opihi (a type of shellfish) and often went alone to the sea to pry the shellfish from the rocks. One day, a large wave swept her away from the rock and the shore. She was certain she would drown, and the world went black. But when she woke, she was on the beach and a stranger was kneeling beside her. He had saved her life. How was she to know that he had shed his shark skin, transforming himself into a human?

She fell in love with him and married him. Her husband kept his true identity a secret until the day Kalei knew she was going to have a child. "Kalei," her husband said. "I must leave you. Our happy time together is over."

"But you will come back?" she asked. "Tonight?"

"No, not tonight," he had answered.

"Then tomorrow?" she asked hopefully.

That is when he told her he was the king of the sharks and must return to his own people, to a place in the ocean where she could never go. "The child will be a boy," he predicted. "Oh, Kalei, promise me that you will keep his true identity a secret so that the people on the island will not fear him and the high chiefs and island king will not be jealous of Nanaue's power."

"What powers will our son have?" she asked.

"He will have the power to be a shark or a man at will," answered the husband. "That is why you must keep a second promise. Never allow him to taste flesh. Feed him only fish and vegetables, never meat. If he tastes meat, one day he will develop a craving for it that will be so strong that the awful transformation from man to shark will begin."

Kalei promised her husband these two things. "For all these years, I have kept my word," Kalei told Nanaue. But Nanaue's proud old grandfather had not made any promise. He wished Nanaue to become a great warrior. Secretly, since Nanaue had been a small child, the old man had been feeding his grandson dog meat and pork so that he would grow strong. The kapu, or taboo, had long ago been broken.

To please his mother, Nanaue continued to wear his kapa and to stay close to his mother's home. During the day, he worked in her taro and sweet potato gardens. He was a young man now, and busybodies on the island began to talk about him. Why did he never remove his kapa? Why did he never go barebacked like the other young men? And why did he think he was so much better than the other young people that he would not join them in their games and pastimes? Never once had Nanaue swum with them in the ocean.

Nanaue did not let their chatter bother him. He pretended to be friendly. Whenever a person passed the garden, Nanaue asked, "Where are you going?" "To fish," some answered. "To bathe," others said. If the person was alone, Nanaue warned them, "Take care! Do not disappear head and tail into the shark!" Then, after the person had continued to the sea, Nanaue slipped away out of the hot sun.

SOON THE VILLAGERS began to notice a strange coincidence. People who had gone alone to the sea to fish or to bathe did not return again. Their bodies were never found. Some busybodies who had heard Nanaue's warning suspected him of wrongdoing. But they could prove nothing.

One day, 'Umi, the king of Hawai'i, ordered all young men to work on his large plantation. Nanaue did not go. The busybodies were shocked at such bold disobedience. They reported Nanaue to the king's warriors. The warriors came to Kalei's garden and dragged Nanaue before the king. 'Umi eyed the young man standing before him, wearing a *kapa* even though the day was very hot. Nanaue was tall and broad-shouldered. The king knew at once that he would make a fine warrior. Still, he refused to treat him differently from the others and ordered Nanaue to work in the field. Nanaue had no choice but to obey.

In the field, he worked beside the others but did not remove his kapa. "Look at him," a young man said. "He wears a *kapa*! Have you ever seen Nanaue without a *kapa*?"

"Let us pull it off now," another young man said. The jealous workers snatched Nanaue's *kapa* from his shoulders. They laughed and ran away. But suddenly, all were silent. Everybody turned to stare. On Nanaue's back was a great shark's jaw.

"Give it back!" Nanaue shouted at the two boys who had snatched away the cloth. "Give it back to me now!" As he shouted, the jaws on his back seemed to move. The villagers gasped. It was true! Nanaue was a shark-man! He had killed the others. The angry crowd crushed around him.

Maddened, Nanaue whirled about. The jaws on his back snapped and clicked. He bit those who tried to pin him on the ground. He rolled and kicked the way a shark thrashes its tail in the water. But the villagers had ropes, and they lashed his arms and legs. The only way to kill a supernatural shark-man, they knew, was by fire. Within minutes, a large bonfire smoked and sparked on the cliff overlooking the sea.

Nanaue cried for help from the father he had never seen or known. Deep in the ocean cavern, Kamohoali'i heard his son's pleas. Suddenly, Nanaue felt a great power surging inside him. As the flames of the bonfire leaped into the sky, the shark-man burst the ropes that held him. He propelled himself through the angry mob and fled for the cliff. Below, the ocean waves crashed against the rocks. Nanaue jumped. He disappeared into the foaming surf. When he surfaced moments later, he had transformed himself into a shark. He rolled on his back, then, thrashing his great tail, swam out to sea.

The fire still burned. The villagers turned their anger now on Kalei and the old grandfather. They were the ones who had raised the monster. They must be destroyed. But King 'Umi stepped forward and silenced the villagers. "Kalei, what do you have to say about your son?"

"I have kept my promise to my husband, the shark god. My son has never tasted meat!"

"It is a lie!" cried the crowd. "She lies! She must be destroyed!"

Just then, the proud old grandfather spoke up. "I did it. I secretly broke the *kapu* and fed my grandson the forbidden food."

King 'Umi listened. Kamohoali'i was a powerful god. He must have loved Kalei to have married her and fathered a son. It was not Nanaue's fault that the grandfather had broken the *kapu*. These were the thoughts of the king. "Old man," he said, "you were wrong not to obey the shark god. The first wrongdoing was yours, not the boy's. Therefore, Nanaue shall be banished forever from the island." Then, not wanting to anger the greatest of all shark gods, the king ordered the villagers to free Kalei and the old grandfather.

Kalei returned to her home, a sad and lonely woman. She had lost both a husband and a son.

Alone, Nanaue swam from island to island. One day, he saw a beautiful girl alone on the beach. Just as his father had done years ago, Nanaue rescued the girl from drowning. Like his father, also, he hid the secret of his true identity underneath his *kapa*. He told the villagers he was a stranger from Hawai'i, and they accepted him. Soon the pretty girl became his wife. For a time, Nanaue was happy. But the craving for flesh returned, and the transformation from man to shark began again.

"Take care!" Nanaue warned the people going down to the sea. "Take care you do not disappear head and tail into the shark!"

ONCE MORE the strange disappearances began. The frightened villagers stopped all fishing and swimming. It was not safe to go into even the shallowest water. Finally, they asked a *kahuna*, a shark priest, for advice. The *kahuna* told them, "Be ready with your nets the next time Nanaue gives his peculiar warning."

They did not have to wait long. The next morning, just as Nanaue said, "Take care!" the villagers ambushed him. They tore his *kapa* from his shoulders and threw the fishing nets over him. Nanaue fought wildly. He whirled and thrashed on the beach, but his turning and twisting only tangled the net more tightly around him. The people beat him with stones and bamboo canes while others hurried to gather brush and wood to build a bonfire on Kainalu Hill.

Nanaue lay bleeding on the beach, caught in a web of nets. As each wave broke onto the shore, it washed a little closer to Nanaue's bound feet. If he could only reach the water, he could transform himself again into a powerful shark. Another wave rolled over the shore. Nanaue stretched, but the water slipped back into the sea again.

On the hill, the fire brightened the sky. Just as another larger wave broke on shore, the villagers dragged Nanaue away in the wet sand. His struggles now were weak. His body gouged a deep gully in the ground as they hauled him up the side of the hill toward the flames.

Kamohoali'i did not come to his son's rescue that day. Who knows why? Perhaps he was disappointed that his son could not control his terrible cravings. Perhaps he was angry that Nanaue had not learned from his past experiences. That day, Nanaue died in the fire on Kainalu Hill. The shallow ravine that his body made in the ground still remains. The place is known even today as Pu'umano, or Shark Hill.

Chapter Five

The Night of the Crying Trees

The people of the South Pacific islands have long shared

their ocean world with sharks. Many island cultures both worshiped sharks as gods and feared them as demons. Myths and legends surrounded these sacred sharks. This story is a retelling of a myth that comes from the people who live on the Solomon Islands, a group of thirty islands in the southwest Pacific Ocean.

I N TAKOLA VILLAGE, the people sing the story of Gaitani. On the night he was born, they say, the shade trees crossed their branches and rasped against each other. The sound the trees made in the wind was like a baby crying. It traveled deep below the ocean to the mouths of the caverns where the shark gods were sleeping. The great fishes woke and climbed to the water's surface to listen. Miles and miles away near the island of Guadalcanal, the strongest of all the shark gods—Beasavu—stopped his midnight hunting to wonder what wild creature was being born this night.

The child born near the pool beyond the village was not a human child. It was a shark-child. As the mother gazed upon her son for the first time, the trees above her cried again in the wind. "I will name him after this sound," said Kosagoa, the mother. "I will call him Gaitani."

She slipped her newborn son under the silver skin of moonlight on the pool. At once, Gaitani began to swim vigorously.

Each day, Kosagoa came from the village to the pool to look upon her son. A year passed, and another. Gaitani fed on the fish in the pool and became stronger. In a few years, Gaitani had grown into a huge shark. The small fish in the pool no longer satisfied his appetite. He began to attack the villagers who passed too close to the pool's shore.

Frightened, the villagers went to Gaitani's uncle and demanded that something be done. Kosagoa knew that her son had outgrown his human home. She knew the villagers and Gaitani's uncle were right—Gaitani must leave.

Although Gaitani was banished from the silver pool, he did not change his bad habits. He swam along the dark ocean bottom, listening for the beating sounds of swimmers in the surf. Then rising swiftly, he attacked and ate his fill. From island to island he roamed. Always he surprised, then killed, the people.

By now, Beasavu was an old shark. But he remembered the night of the crying trees. When Gaitani appeared in the waters around Guadalcanal, Beasavu knew the time had come to fight the fierce, young shark. A great battle began. When it had ended, Beasavu was no longer the strongest of the sacred shark gods. Gaitani had defeated him.

As the victor, Gaitani stole Beasavu's wife. Together they returned to the island of Gaitani's birth. At first, the villagers of Takola were alarmed to see that Gaitani was once more swimming in the waters offshore. But Gaitani was not the same voracious shark he had been as a youth. He had proven himself the strongest of the sacred shark gods. He was content now. Never again did he attack his own people.

PART III
THE
SCAVENGERS

Chapter Six

Shark Killer

from Shark! Shark!
by William E. Young

The Hawaiians had a name for him—*kano mano,* shark killer. Others called him Sharky Bill. He preferred to call himself a pioneer shark hunter. His real name was William E. Young.

In 1920 the Ocean Leather Company, which made boots and belts out of sharksin, hired Young to capture sharks. When his employer asked him how far he was willing to go to hunt sharks, Young answered, "To the ends of the earth." For thirty years, in the Pacific and the Atlantic oceans, from Africa to Australia, Captain Young made shark hunting his business, taking as many as thirty sharks in a single day. When he finally retired, Captain Young guessed he probably had killed more than 100,000 sharks in all.

He had come to the South Pacific with his brother in 1900 to start a fishing business. At first, the Young brothers earned money by hauling garbage from Honolulu into the deeper ocean and dumping it. That's when they saw the sharks. Carcasses of horses were often part of the dumped garbage, and the sharks tore madly at the carrion, devouring it as it sank out of sight.

The sharks fascinated Young. He was determined to find out as much as he could about the scavengers. He began casting around the islands for shark stories. Boastful sailors told him tall tales of tricking and outswimming the sharks. The Kanakas, or Hawaiian natives, told him ancient myths of 'aumakua and of shark-men born with jaws on their backs. These stories were the beginning of Young's education about shark behavior.

Why was Young so curious about sharks? Ambition. He had no intention of hauling garbage all of his life. He believed that big money could be made from hunting sharks. He got the idea one day while fishing with his brother and some Kanakas. Many years later he and Horace S. Mazet wrote about that day in a book called *Shark! Shark!* Published in 1934, it was the first book entirely about sharks. The story that follows is taken from that book.

"*Mano! Mano!*—Shark! Shark!" the Kanakas would call as they spotted the sharks circling around the ships…waiting for the free meals the ship provided when garbage was thrown overboard. Often the clear water was alive with hungry sharks. The cry of Kanakas rang in my ears. "*Mano! Mano!*" Finally I went to the side of the ship and leaned over the railing.

There they were, the savage, armored sea tigers which had become my fetish [obsession], my totem. I thrilled to the sight. As I leaned there, staring in utter fascination, my throat constricted. Tingling shivers ran up and down my spine, to my fingertips and toes. I wished for a harpoon, a rifle, anything that would give me a chance to make my first shark kill. I was like a boy with buck fever, and I resolved that we would catch a shark just as soon as the opportunity presented itself.

I told one of the English-speaking Kanakas aboard that I wanted to catch a shark. "*Mano?*" he asked, looking at me curiously. "Yes, mano," I replied. The Kanaka disappeared in the direction of the galley and soon returned with a big piece of salt pork, a stout line and a great hook. He was jabbering wildly with excitement. "*Hana paa mano*—we'll catch that shark and make him fast. He too much *wiki wiki kau kau haole*—he will eat a white man very, very quick."

40

He and another Kanaka cast the line into the sea. The moment it struck the water it was seized. Mano was hooked! One of the boys borrowed a meat hook from the cook, got into a small boat alongside, and hooked the shark through the mouth.

Up came the dripping monster, thrashing his tail and making the boat falls [ropes] shiver and vibrate. Quickly another line was secured around the shark's tail. Now the great fish hung suspended within reach of the rail.

Swish! The glint of a heavy knife caught my eye. The native hacked off the shark's tail. The rest of the boys danced with joy and hurled what I presume were epithets [curses] at the crippled foe like a group of children. At a word, the falls were slacked off. The boy in the boat cut the hook from the cruel mouth, and the shark was free. Free—for a living death. If he were not immediately devoured by his fellows he would soon become weak from loss of blood and feebly wiggle his last a short time later. . . . This one died at the jaws of other sharks. Killed by shark and man, by hunger and vengeance.

One less mano, I thought, but what is one more or less when the seven seas are full of these scavengers? Truly, here was a happy hunting ground, if only for the price a Chinaman would pay for the sharkfin from which he makes his delectable soup. But we were to discover that there is more in shark hunting than just fins. The thought—and the persistent desire to catch sharks—never left me.

O N THE SHORES of Lake Nicaragua, a burial is taking place. The dead man is an Indian from a village that lies a short way into the forest. Why the man has died is not so important to this story. How he will be buried is.

The villagers dress the dead man in feathers and in emerald and gold jewelry. They carry his body down from the hillside to a quiet cove on the lake, a place called Playa de los Muertos, the Beach of the Dead. They lay the dead man in a boat, then pole the boat away from shore to where the water is very clear and deep. The men lift the body, heavy now in death and jewels, and drop it overboard. As the corpse sinks silently, a shark rises swiftly from the depths of the lake to investigate. The men in the boat do not wait to see what will happen next. Their role in this solemn ceremony is over, and they return to shore. The dead man belongs now to the sharks.

Unknown to the villagers, other eyes have witnessed the burial. The Dutchman is an adventurer who has come to Nicaragua not to kill sharks, but to find his fortune in gold. In the city of San Carlos, the Dutchman heard stories of a village chief who had discovered gold in the hills surrounding Lake Nicaragua. So much gold was in the hills that the native Indians buried their dead in gold!

Gold. That was why the Dutchman has traveled across the lake, stopping at every village. Other prospectors had gone into the hills before him. No doubt they, too, had heard the stories of the old chief. But they always returned empty-handed.

THE DUTCHMAN, too, might have returned with nothing if he had not camped one night on the shore of a quiet cove. He had no way of knowing that he had come ashore at Playa de los Muertos, for the place could not be foundon any map. What he witnessed there changed his way of thinking about gold. And about sharks.

Hidden in the thick bushes along the water's edge, the Dutchman watched the villagers carry the dead man down to the lakeshore. He saw the glint of emeralds and gold that covered the body. And, after the Indians had cast the body into the lake and disappeared again into the forest, the Dutchman saw the dorsal fin of a shark circling the area where the burial had been.

The Dutchman got an idea. The others failed to find gold, because they did not know that the gold was buried in the bellies of the sharks! Digging was one way to prospect for gold, he thought. Fishing might be another. It was a mad idea, for there were hundreds of sharks in the lake. Still, he baited a fishing line, then shoved his boat from shore. Bull sharks are large and strong, and they fight hard when hooked on a line. But, as the Dutchman found out, even bull sharks can be caught and killed and hauled back to shore. There, the Dutchman slit open the shark's gray-white belly and recovered the emeralds and gold. He dumped the slaughtered shark back into the lake. Almost at once, other sharks came to feed upon it. That is how the Dutchman got his second idea.

Deeper in the forest was a deep stream. Here the Dutchman built a crude hut. The villagers took notice of him, but they were not concerned. Other men had come into the hills to search for gold. The Dutchman was just one more. Weeks passed, then months. Each time the villagers buried their dead, the Dutchman later went down to the lake and fished for gold. Between burials, he hunted other animals and dumped their carcasses into the creek, hoping to entice the sharks to swim upstream.

Perhaps that was when the Indians found him out. Perhaps one day while the Dutchman was away from camp, they entered his hut and discovered the pile of gold and jewels that he had robbed from the dead. Sacrificing their dead to the sharks was an old custom. It was a way to satisfy the man-eaters so that the living might remain safe. What the Dutchman had done was trickery. Worse, he had disturbed the sacred dead.

The Indians retreated into the forest to wait. When the Dutchman returned, they captured him. They could have sent him to the bottom of the lake, but the Dutchman was not good enough for the sharks. Instead, they set fire to his hut and cut the Dutchman's throat.

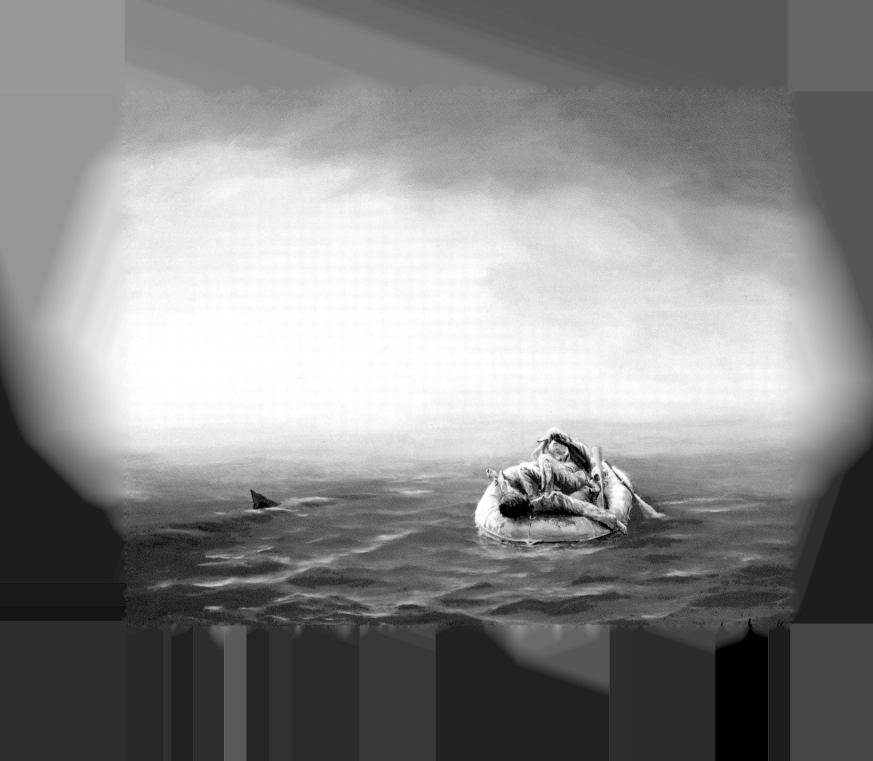

Chapter Eight

Four Days at Sea

The Loss of the U.S.S. Indianapolis

In 1941, World War II exploded in the South Pacific. Servicemen painted shark jaws on the noses of American fighter planes and bombers. The sharks on these fighting machines were predators whose strikes were swift and deadly. The jaws were meant to frighten the enemy and to inspire bravery in the pilot and crew.

With heavy fighting came casualties. Torpedoed ships and downed planes brought thousands of fighting men into contact with deep-sea sharks. In the sky, shark jaws might have inspired boldness. In the ocean, they triggered fear and panic. These jaws were not paint on steel. They were real. The true story that follows is based on eyewitness accounts.

*W*hat happened in the South Pacific at 12:14 A.M. on Monday, July 30, 1945, was very unusual and very tragic. The U.S.S. *Indianapolis* was cruising through the Philippine Sea. Just after midnight, the first of two Japanese torpedoes struck the ship. The first tore through the front of the ship. The second ripped away sections of the ship's bottom and knocked out the communication system, making it impossible for the crew to radio for help. Twelve minutes later, the cruiser sank.

Many men died in the explosions. Others were unable to abandon ship before it sank. About eight hundred men managed to escape. But their struggle for survival in the water was just beginning.

In the few minutes between the explosions and the sinking of the heavy cruiser, a few life rafts had been cut away and thrown into the water. Most rafts could hold as many as twenty men each. The floor of each raft was made of heavy ropes with wooden slats. To keep dry, the men had to sit on the sides. Those men unable to reach a raft clung to whatever floating debris they could grab—a crate, a toilet seat. Still others had nothing to hold on to at all. Some of these men had life vests. Others did not.

During the night, wind and the ocean currents pulled the survivors at different speeds. The men in the rafts drifted in a 10-knot (18-kilometer) wind. The men floating in the water were carried more slowly by the currents. The result was that by daylight the survivors were scattered over miles of open ocean. Some men found each other and grouped together for safety.

(2.5-centimeter) knife, stabbed a shark in the head. The shark lashed violently with its tail, knocking the man into the sea and nearly capsizing the raft. The others managed to drag the sailor back onto the raft.

By the time the sun rose on the fourth day, fewer than half of the eight hundred survivors were still alive.

*L*ieutenant Marks was flying a PBY, a type of naval seaplane, on a patrolling mission over the Philippine Sea when he received word on his radio that some thirty "floaters" had been spotted in the ocean. He changed course for the location given. What he saw as he flew over the area was not thirty men in the water, but at least one hundred fifty of the survivors. Even from the sky, he could tell that they were in bad shape. Even from the sky, he could see the dorsal fins of sharks.

Although Marks had never made a sea landing, he decided he had no choice but to try. The men in the water might not last until rescue ships arrived to pick them up. He circled for a landing. His PBY skimmed the waves, then bounced with three hard jolts that damaged the plane's body. Marks motored the PBY from one floating survivor to another. He and his crew picked up as many men as the plane could carry, laying them side by side in the cargo hold. But even then, Marks refused to give up. His crew rescued more men, laying them on top of the plane's wings.

Marks knew his PBY was too damaged to fly again. But at least the plane could provide some shelter and safety from the sharks until the rescue ships could arrive. The first ship cruised into the area after midnight. Help had come at last. But for many, it had come too late. Of the approximately eight hundred men who had escaped the sinking *Indianapolis*, only 318 men had survived the four days at sea.

"It is a terrible thing to be attacked by a shark," says shark researcher Doctor David Baldridge, a retired United States Navy captain. During the war, he was almost commissioned to the U.S.S. *Indianapolis*, and he knew at least one man aboard who had died in the jaws of a shark. "But the sharks were not being bad guys," Dr. Baldridge says. Many of the men died from wounds suffered during the explosion and from four days in the ocean without food and drinking water. The dead and the dying became prey of opportunity for the sharks. "The sharks did what any wild animal must do," says Dr. Baldridge, "in order to survive."

*S*hark Sense was a handbook published by the United States Navy in March 1944. The purpose of the book was to teach pilots and sailors about sharks and what to do if attacked by one. The book began with this sentence: "Men who know most about sharks are the men who fear them the least." There is a lot of truth in that statement. And some of the book's advice was sound, like this passage: "The main hurdle to take concerning sharks—should you be adrift in a life jacket or rubber boat in shark-infested waters—is the mental hazard." In other words, panic is a greater enemy than sharks.

Chapter Nine

The First Shark

from The Old Man and the Sea
by Ernest Hemingway

The short novel *The Old Man and the Sea* tells the story of a Cuban fisherman who catches and kills a giant marlin. It is a dream fish, a fish that could bring the old man fame and some wealth. But to catch such a magnificent fish, the old man has gone too far out to sea. Now, he must bring his prize fish back to shore. In this excerpt from the novel, the first shark picks up the scent.

BLUE SHARK

THE SHARK was not an accident. He had come up from deep down in the water as the dark cloud of blood had settled and dispersed in the mile deep sea. He had come up so fast and absolutely without caution that he broke the surface of the blue water and was in the sun. Then he fell back into the sea and picked up the scent and started swimming on the course the skiff and the fish had taken.

Sometimes he lost the scent. But he would pick it up again, or have just a trace of it, and he swam fast and hard on the course. He was a very big Mako shark built to swim as fast as the fastest fish in the sea and everything about him was beautiful except his jaws. His back was as blue as a sword fish's and his belly was silver and his hide was smooth and handsome. He was built as a sword fish except for his huge jaws which were tight shut now as he swam fast, just under the surface with his high dorsal fin knifing through the water without wavering. Inside the closed double lip of his jaws all of his eight rows of teeth were slanted inwards. They were not the ordinary pyramid-shaped teeth of most sharks. They were shaped like a man's fingers when they are crisped like claws. They were nearly as long as the fingers of the old man and they had razor-sharp cutting edges on both sides. This was a fish built to feed on all the fishes in the sea, that were so fast and strong and well armed that they had not other enemy. Now he speeded up as he smelled the fresher scent and his blue dorsal fin cut the water.

When the old man saw him coming he knew that this was a shark that had no fear at all and would do exactly what he wished. He prepared the harpoon and made the rope fast while he watched the shark come on. The rope was short as it lacked what he had cut away to lash the fish.

The old man's head was clear and good now and he was full of resolution but he had little hope. It was too good to last, he thought. He took one look at the great fish as he watched the shark close in. It might as well have been a dream, he thought. I cannot keep him from hitting me but maybe I can get him. *Dentuso,* he thought. Bad luck to your mother.

The shark closed fast astern and when he hit the fish the old man saw his mouth open and his strange eyes and the clicking chop of the teeth as he drove forward in the meat just above the tail. The shark's head was out of water and his back was coming out and the old man could hear the noise of skin and flesh ripping on the big fish when he rammed the harpoon down onto the shark's head at a spot where the line between his eyes intersected with the line that ran straight back from his nose. There were no such lines. There was only the heavy sharp blue head and the big eyes and the clicking, thrusting all-swallowing jaws. But that was the location of the brain and the old man hit it. He hit it with his blood mushed hands driving a good harpoon with all his strength. He hit it without hope but with resolution and complete malignancy.

The shark swung over and the old man saw his eye was not alive and then he swung over once again, wrapping himself in two loops of the rope. The old man knew that he was dead but the shark would not accept it. Then, on his back, with his tail lashing and his jaws clicking, the shark plowed over the water as a speedboat does. The water was white where his tail beat it and three-quarters of his body was clear above the water when the rope came taut, shivered, and then snapped. The shark lay quietly for a little while on the surface and the old man watched him. Then he went down very slowly.

"He took about forty pounds," the old man said aloud. He took my harpoon too and all the rope, he thought, and now my fish bleeds again and there will be others.

He did not like to look at the fish anymore since he had been mutilated. When the fish had been hit it was as though he himself were hit.

But I killed the shark that hit my fish, he thought. And he was the biggest *dentuso* that I have ever seen. And God knows that I have seen big ones.

It was too good to last, he thought. I wish it had been a dream now and that I had never hooked the fish and was alone in bed on the newspapers.

"But man is not made for defeat," he said. "A man can be destroyed but not defeated." I am sorry that I killed the fish though, he thought. Now the bad time is coming and I do not even have the harpoon. The *dentuso* is cruel and able and strong and intelligent. But I was more intelligent than he was. Perhaps not, he thought. Perhaps I was only better armed.

PART IV

THE
PREDATORS

Chapter Ten

Watson and the Shark

by Brook Watson, the London Advertiser, 1778

He was a sailor. In high winds during a storm at sea, he fell overboard. His mates tossed him a lifeline and began to haul him back to the ship. Suddenly, a monster fish appeared from below the surface. As his mates watched, the fish attacked the sailor and tore him to pieces. They could do nothing to save him. Later, a shipmate described the attack in a letter dated 1580. That letter eventually became Case #462 in the International Shark Attack File. It is perhaps the first-ever eyewitness report of a shark attack.

*t*he story of "Watson and the Shark" is similar to Case #462. Watson was fourteen years old when a shark attacked him in the harbor of Havana, Cuba, in 1749.

Watson, however, survived and later hired the American painter John Singleton Copley to capture the dramatic attack on canvas. Today, the painting hangs in the National Gallery in Washington, D.C. The story that follows is Watson's own eyewitness account of the attack, the story from which Copley created his painting.

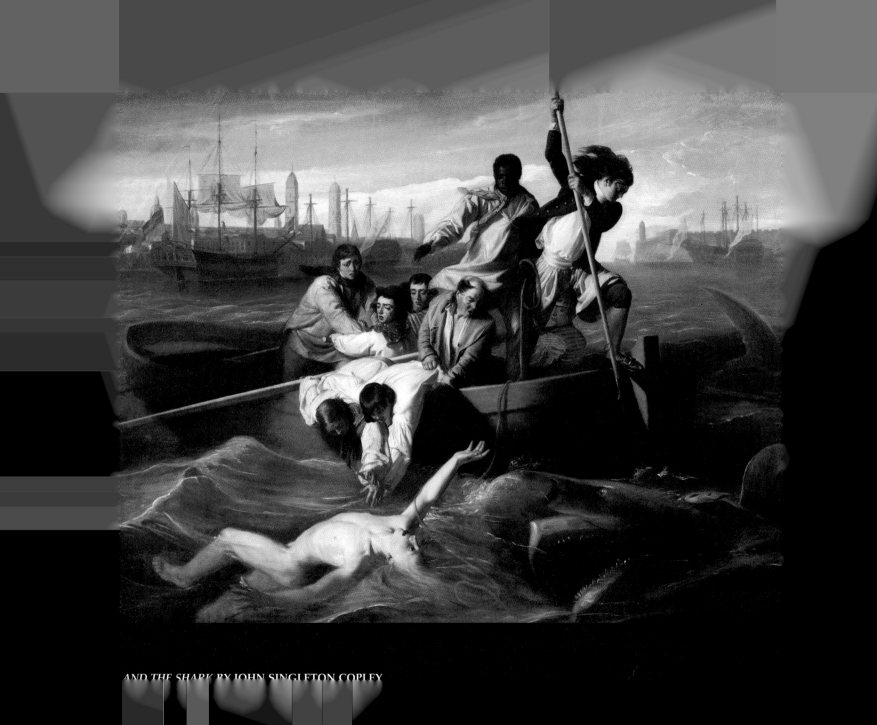

AND THE SHARK BY JOHN SINGLETON COPLEY

BROOK WATSON, merchant, now resident in the city of London, being in Havana when a youth of fourteen years, was amusing himself one day by swimming about a merchant ship whilst it lay at anchor. Being the ship was a distance of about 200 yards from shore, a few shipmates were waiting in a small boat to take the captain ashore. Suddenly they were struck with horror upon perceiving a shark making towards young Watson as his devoted prey. The monster was already too near him for the youth to be timely apprised of his danger; and the sailors had the afflicted sight of seeing him seized and precipitated down the flood with his voracious assailant, before they could put off to attempt his deliverance. They however hastened towards the place where they—young Watson and the shark—had disappeared. Anxiously, they expected to see the body rise. In about two minutes they discovered the body rise at about a hundred yards distance, but ere they could reach him, he was second time seized by the shark, and again sunk from their sight. The sailors now took the precaution to place a man in the bow of the boat, provided with a hook to strike the fish, should it appear within reach, and repeat its attempt at seizing the body. In less than two minutes they discovered the youth on the surface of the water,

65

and the monster still in eager pursuit of him. At the very instant he was about to be seized the third time, the shark was struck with the boat hook, and driven from his prey....

Suffice it to say, in regard to the singular fate of Mr. Watson, the shark seized him both times by the right leg; in the first attack, all the flesh was stripped off the bone from the calf downwards; in the second, the foot was divided from the leg by the ankle. By the skill of the surgeon, and the aid of a good habit of body, after suffering an amputation of the limb a little below the knee, the youth who was thus wonderfully and literally saved from the jaws of death, received a perfect cure in about three months.

Eleven

The Summer of the Shark

In 1916 a number of shark attacks along the New Jersey coast *opened a new chapter* on understanding shark behavior. Until that summer, many people in the United States believed that a shark could not kill a human. Dr. Frederick A. Lucas, director of the American Museum of Natural History in New York City, told newspaper reporters that a shark's jaws were not strong enough to bite through a human legbone.

Dr. Lucas was wrong.

This story comes from eyewitness accounts and newspaper articles.

GREAT WHITE SHARKS

SPRING LAKE is a small resort town on the New Jersey seacoast. On July 6, 1916, hundreds of men, women, and children were on the beach, enjoying the Fourth of July holiday week. Suddenly, a cry for help came from the water. The two lifeguards on duty spotted a swimmer in trouble, far beyond the roped-off swimming area. Quickly, they launched a lifeboat and rowed hard over the waves for the swimmer. On shore, the crowd watched in fear.

The man in trouble was Charles Bruder. He was a twenty-three-year-old bellboy in one of the large hotels that faced the ocean. Young and athletic, he often took a long swim before going to work. That Wednesday morning was not the first time he had gone beyond the lifelines. As the lifeboat neared him, Bruder shrieked loudly again. The water around him was red with his blood. "Shark—shark got me!" Bruder gasped. Then he lost consciousness.

As the guards dragged him into the boat, they saw that Bruder's left leg had been bitten off above the knee. Emergency treatment failed. Charles Bruder died minutes later on the beach.

The *New York Times* ran the story on page one with this headline: "Shark Kills Bather Off Jersey Beach." The article described the details of Bruder's death. The story ended by mentioning that a similar attack had occurred five days earlier farther south, at Beach Haven, New Jersey. The victim in that attack was Charles Vansant. He, too, had died from the bites of a shark.

Two shark attacks and two deaths within one week was extraordinary. It had never happened before anywhere along the New Jersey coastline. Additional newspaper articles in the days that followed tried to explain the phenomenon. A scarcity of fish, it was reported, had prompted the attacks. The sharks along the Jersey coast were "desperate for hunger," the papers said. The articles quoted Dr. Frederick A. Lucas. He pointed out that a person had a greater chance of being struck by lightning than of being attacked by a shark. But lightning had already struck twice, and people were frightened.

Summer vacationers provided valuable business for the hotels and shops in Spring Lake, and the mayor of the town took immediate action to ease everyone's fears. He ordered workers to enclose the swimming area with a wire net to keep sharks out. The work took about a week to complete. Meanwhile, men armed with rifles patrolled the area beyond the lifelines in motorboats. Despite dragging hunks of lamb in the water behind the boats, no sharks took the bait. For the time being, it looked as if the shark threat was over.

MATAWAN CREEK is a narrow, shallow stream. It links the small town of Matawan, New Jersey, with the Atlantic Ocean, 11 miles (18 kilometers) to the east. It is a tidal creek. As the ocean tides rise and fall twice a day, so does the level of the creek water. Along the creek was an old steamboat dock. In 1916 steamboats no longer traveled on Matawan Creek, and the dock and the cool water under it had become a popular swimming spot for the boys in town. Six days after Charles Bruder died from a shark attack at Spring Lake, Thomas Cottrell saw something in Matawan Creek that alarmed him. He was crossing a bridge over the water when he spied a huge, dark shadow moving swiftly upstream. Cottrell was a retired sailor. He knew sharks were saltwater fish. and one couldn't be this far inland. Even so, he knew what he had seen. He hurried into town to alert the people that a shark was in the creek. No one believed him. They laughed and called him a crazy old sailor.

Meanwhile, at the steamboat dock, twelve-year-old Lester Stilwell was floating in the deepest part of the creek, almost midstream. His friends, who were closer to the pier, saw Lester suddenly disappear under the water. When he surfaced, he screamed and waved his arms wildly. Then, swirling around in a flurry of water, he disappeared beneath the surface again. His friends ran for help.

One of the first people to hear the boys shouting was Stanley Fisher. He was young and had just opened a dry-cleaning business in town. The boys were yelling that Lester had taken a fit in the creek. Fisher didn't hesitate. He ran to the creek. Some accounts of the story say that a woman teacher warned Fisher that a shark might be in the creek. His answer was, "A shark here? I don't care—I'm going after that boy."

On the dock, Fisher pulled off his clothes and jumped into the water. He swam to midstream and dove—once, twice. On the third try, he surfaced and cried, "I've got it!" By now, other townsfolk had crowded to the creek bank. A few had pushed rowboats into the water. With his arm around Lester's body, Fisher swam toward the opposite bank. Just as he touched bottom and stood, Lester's body slipped away from him and under the water again. The next moment, Fisher was dragged under as well.

"The shark! The shark!" cried the crowd on shore. The men in the rowboats pulled hard for the spot where Fisher had disappeared. Once more, Fisher surfaced. But the child was not in his arms. Fisher stumbled onto the muddy bank and collapsed. The men who reached him first saw that the flesh on Fisher's right leg had been raked from above the hip to below the knee. He was bleeding heavily. A local doctor applied a tourniquet, using rope from one of the rowboats.

Fisher was still conscious. He had seen the shark, he told them. It was clinging to his leg. Those who had witnessed the attack from the steamboat dock later told reporters that they had seen the white belly of a shark rolling to the surface as it seized Fisher and yanked him under.

The nearest hospital was miles away. The men made a crude stretcher from old planks and carried Fisher to an automobile that would take him to the Matawan railroad station. In less than three hours, Fisher was wheeled into an operating room at Monmouth Memorial Hospital. But it was too late. Fisher had lost too much blood. He died before doctors could begin the operation.

Two more people had died. The newspaper reporters swarmed into Matawan with notebooks and cameras. Hundreds of people from the town—men, women, even children—lined the banks, ready to do battle. They were armed with dynamite, shotguns, handguns, harpoons, pitchforks, even hammers. They spread fishing nets across the creek to trap the shark. It was as if Nanaue, the shark man of Hawaii, had suddenly reappeared in Matawan Creek. Like the ancient Hawaiians, the people of Matawan wanted one thing—revenge.

The July 13 edition of *The New York Times* described the town's reaction to the shark attacks this way:

> Tonight the whole town is stirred by a personal feeling, a feeling which makes men and women regard the fish as they might a human being who had taken the lives of a boy and youth and badly, perhaps mortally, injured another youngster. The one purpose in which everybody shares is to get the shark, to kill it, and to see its body drawn up on shore, where all may look and be assured it will destroy no more.

The other "youngster" mentioned in the article was fourteen-year-old Joseph Dunn. He, too, had been swimming in the creek that hot summer afternoon. But he was farther downstream. When someone warned him to get out of the water because a shark had attacked a boy at the steamboat dock, Joseph Dunn swam at once toward shore. According to newspaper reports, a shark grabbed his leg before he could clear the water. "I felt my leg going down the shark's throat," Dunn later told a reporter. "I thought it would swallow me." Dunn escaped by kicking the shark in the snout. The shark let go, and Dunn climbed to the safety of the shore.

For TWO DAYS, men in rowboats poled the muddy creek bottom, searching for Lester Stilwell's body. Hour after hour, sticks of dynamite exploded in the creek, sending geysers of water and dead fish into the air. But neither Lester's body nor the shark's were stunned to the surface.

Newspapers spread rumors of the shark sightings. "SHARK BREAKS NET, FLEES TO SEA" was the headline in *The New York American* on July 15, 1916. The story reported: "Bucking the line like a football halfback, a giant shark plunged through the chicken wire net that penned it in at Matawan Creek and escaped to the ocean last night."

Sensational news stories like this triggered a wave of shark killings along the coast and even as far as a mile out into the ocean. "A new sport, combined with a public service—the hunting of sharks, has sprung up!" reported *The New York Times* on July 14. That same day a 8.5-foot (2.6-meter) great white shark was killed in Raritan Bay, just 4 miles (6.5 kilometers) from the mouth of Matawan Creek. Was it the same shark that had attacked Lester Stillwell and Stanley Fisher? No one knows for certain.

It is also unclear whether Lester Stilwell's body was ever found. One newspaper reported that two men from Matawan found Stilwell's body upstream against the creek bank on July 15. The seven bite marks on his body proved that he had indeed been bitten by a shark. But other sources don't agree. A different newspaper reported that the body was found months later. Still another wrote, "It is believed that the child was literally torn to pieces and devoured." Exaggeration, even in newspapers, can often cloud the truth, however, especially when the story is about a shark attack.

After Charles Bruder's death at Spring Lake, Dr. Lucas had told reporters that a shark's jaws could not bite through a human legbone. After the attacks at Matawan Creek, he changed his opinion somewhat. "I never said sharks never attacked men," he told reporters now. "They do so rarely. But," he added, "under stress of hunger, sharks become bold."

He offered this final theory to explain the extraordinary shark attacks. Destruction by insects and animals often happens in cycles. Some summers are locust years. The jumping insects travel in swarms, destroying farmers' crops. Some summers are butterfly years or army-worm years.

The year 1916, concluded Dr. Lucas, was the summer of the shark.

BRONZE WHALER SHARK AND MACKEREL

Chapter Twelve

Ghost Dance

from Kon-Tiki
by Thor Heyerdahl

Five men set out on an adventure: to cross the South Pacific Ocean on a raft that they named *Kon-Tiki*. Almost from the start, dolphins and sharks were curious companions in the water around the raft. The crew got used to the sharks and often played a tug-of-war game by catching them by their tails. One night, long into their voyage, they encountered a species of shark that startled their imaginations, a mysterious sea monster unlike any fish they had ever seen.

THE SEA CONTAINS many surprises for him who has his floor on a level with the surface and drifts along slowly and noiselessly. A sportsman who breaks his way through the woods may come back and say that no wild life is to be seen. Another may sit down on a stump and wait, and often rustlings and cracklings will begin and curious eyes peer out. So it is on the sea, too. Not a day passed as we sat floating on the surface of the sea that a curious guest didn't wriggle and waggle about us. A few of them, such as dolphins and pilot fish, grew so familiar that they accompanied the raft across the sea and kept round us day and night.

When night had fallen and the stars were twinkling in the dark tropical sky, a phosphorescence [shimmering light] flashed around in rivalry with the stars. Single glowing plankton resembled round live coals so vividly that we drew in our bare legs when the glowing pellets were washed up around our feet at the raft's stern. When we caught them, we saw that they were little brightly shining species of shrimp.

On such nights we were sometimes scared when two round shining eyes suddenly rose out of the sea right alongside the raft and glared at us with an unblinking hypnotic stare. The visitors were often big squids which came up and floated on the surface with their devilish green eyes.

We gradually grew accustomed to having these submarine creatures under our floor, but nevertheless we were just as surprised every time a new species appeared.

About two o'clock on a cloudy night, when the man at the helm had difficulty in distinguishing black water from black sky, he caught sight of a faint light illumination down in the water. Slowly it took the shape of a large animal. It was impossible to say whether it was plankton shining on its body or whether the animal itself had a phosphorescent surface. But the glimmer down in the black water gave the ghostly creature wavering outlines. Sometimes it was roundish, sometimes oval or triangular, and suddenly it split into two parts which swam to and fro under the raft independently of each other. Finally, there were three of these large shining phantoms wandering round in slow circles under us.

They were real monsters. The visible parts alone were some five fathoms [6 feet, 9 meters] long, and we all quickly collected on deck and followed the ghost dance. It went on for hour after hour, following the course of the raft. Mysterious and noiseless, our shining companions kept a good way beneath the surface. But often they were right under the raft. The glimmer of their light on their backs revealed that the beasts were bigger than elephants, but they were not whales, for they never came up to breathe. Were they giant ray fish which changed shape when they turned over on their sides? They took no notice at all if we held the light right down on the surface to lure them up so that we might see what kind of creatures they were. And, like all proper goblins and ghosts, they sunk and sunk into the depths when the dawn began to break.

We never got an explanation of this night visit from the three shining monsters. But a day and a half later in the full midday sunshine, we received another mysterious visit. It was May 24, and we were drifting on a leisurely swell. About noon, we had thrown overboard the guts of two big dolphins we had caught earlier in the morning. I was having a refreshing plunge overboard at the bow, lying in the water but keeping a good lookout and hanging on to a rope end, when I caught sight of a thick brown fish, six feet [1.8 meters] long, which came swimming toward me through the crystal-clear sea water. I hopped quickly up on to the edge of the raft and sat in the hot sun looking at the fish as it passed quietly.

Then I heard a wild war whoop from Knut, who was sitting behind the bamboo cabin. He bellowed, "Shark!" till his voice cracked. As we had sharks swimming alongside the raft almost daily without creating such excitement, we all realized that this must be something extra-special.

While I had been lying in the water, Knut had been squatting on the raft, washing his pants in the swell. When he looked up for a moment he was staring straight into the biggest and ugliest face any of us had ever seen in the whole of our lives. It was the head of a sea monster, so huge and so hideous that, if the Old Man of the Sea himself had come up, he could not have made such an impression on us.

The head was broad and flat like a frog's, with two small eyes right at the sides, and a toadlike jaw which was four or five feet [1.2 or 1.5 meters] wide and had long fringes drooping from the corners of the mouth. Behind the head was an enormous body ending in a long thin tail with a pointed tail fin which stood straight up and showed that this sea monster wasn't any kind of whale. The body looked brownish under the water, but both head and body were thickly covered with small white spots.

The monster came quietly, lazily swimming after us from behind. It grinned like a bulldog and lashed gently with its tail. The large round dorsal fin projected clear of the water and sometimes the tail fin as well. When the creature was in the trough of the swell, the water flowed about the broad back as though washing round a submerged reef. In front of the broad jaws swam a whole crowd of zebra-striped pilot fish in fan formation, and large remora fish and other parasites sat firmly attached to the huge body.

The monster was a whale shark, the largest shark and the largest fish known in the world today. It has an average length of fifty feet [15 meters], and according to scientists, it weights fifteen tons. One harpooned baby had a liver weighing six hundred pounds [272 kilograms] and a collection of three thousand teeth in each of its broad jaws.

Our monster was so large that, when it began to swim in circles round us and under our raft, its head was visible on one side while the whole of its tail stuck out on the other. And so grotesque and stupid did it appear when seen fullface that we could not help shouting with laughter. Still, we realized that it had strength enough in its tail to smash the *Kon-Tiki* to pieces if it attacked us. Again and again it made narrower and narrower circles just under the raft. All we could do was wait and see what might happen.

We stood on the raft with hand harpoons ready for action, but they seemed to us like toothpicks in relation to the beast. There was no indication that the whale shark ever thought of leaving us again; it circled round us and followed like a faithful dog, close up to the raft. None of us had ever experienced or thought we should experience anything like it.

The whale shark went on encircling us for barely an hour, but to us the visit seemed to last a whole day. At last it became too exciting for Erik who was standing at the corner of the raft with an 8-foot [2.5 meter] hand harpoon. He raised the harpoon above his head. As the whale shark came gliding slowly toward him and its broad head moved right under the corner of the raft, Erik thrust the harpoon with all his giant strength down between his legs and deep into the whale shark's gristly head.

It was a second or two before the giant understood properly what was happening. Then in a flash the placid half-wit was transformed into a mountain of steel muscles.

We heard a swishing noise as the harpoon line rushed over the edge of the raft. We saw a cascade of water as the giant stood on its head and plunged down into the depths. The three men who were standing nearest were flung about the place, head over heels, and two of them were flayed and burned by the line as it rushed through the air. The thick line, strong enough to hold a boat, was caught up on the side of the raft, but it snapped at once like a piece of twine. A few seconds later, a broken-off harpoon shaft came up to the surface 200 yards [183 meters] away.

A shoal of frightened pilot fish shot off through the water in a desperate attempt to keep up with their lord and master. We waited a long time for the monster to come racing back like an infuriated submarine, but we never saw anything more of him.

GREAT WHITE SHARK

Chapter Thirteen

Spyhopping the Snappa

Charlie Donilon is the skipper of a fishing boat out of Port Judith, Rhode Island. The groups that charter his boat for all-day fishing parties are hunting big game fish. What one fishing party encountered off Block Island in the North Atlantic Ocean during the summer of 1983, however, was more than they had bargained for.

THE SNAPPA had been hours at sea. The fishing boat was drifting with the ocean currents, 10 miles (16 kilometers) south of Block Island, Rhode Island, in the North Atlantic. On board was Captain Charlie Donilon and a party of fishermen who had rented his 35-foot (11-meter) boat for the day. It was July 1983. The ocean was flat calm, almost glassy. Chum, a concoction of ground-up fish and blood, spread out behind the *Snappa* in an oily net about a mile (1.6 kilometers) long. The chum was meant to attract large tuna. But tuna were not the only fish lured by the bloody scent that day.

A long shadow—almost half as long as the *Snappa* itself—glided close to the surface and disappeared under the boat. "Cap!" one of the men shouted. "Did you see that?" Charlie had seen it. He leaned over the port side and waited for the giant shadow to make another pass under the boat. It came swiftly, climbing from the depths. But this time the shadow did not veer away. The head of the great fish broke the surface and rose 3 feet (0.9 meters) out of the water, as high as the boat's transom. For one thrilling moment, Charlie Donilon was eye to eye with a great white shark. Then the fish slipped into the ocean again.

The men on deck were startled. But before they could react, the great white surfaced once more, this time with its jaws open. Again it lifted its head above the water, then closed its mouth on the boat's stern. The shark did not viciously snap its jaws. It did not shake its head from side to side to saw away a hunk of the

Snappa's body. The great white simply mouthed the boat. It moved along the port side, tasting the keel, the bowline, the propeller.

Charlie didn't know it then, but the great white is the only shark that raises its head above the water. Marine scientists call this "spyhopping." Killer whales do it, perhaps when looking for prey. Scientists think great whites may do it for the same reason—to spy on seals lounging on rocks or to scare the prey into the water.

On board the *Snappa,* a few of the men were frightened. The boat was miles from land, and the shark was nearly 16 feet (5 meters) long by their guess. "Get us out of here, Cap," they said. But Charlie didn't want to run away. All of his life he had dreamed of one day seeing a great white shark. This was the day. The great white had surprised him, though. Sleek and graceful, it behaved nothing at all like the bloodthirsty, shipwrecking monster-fish in the best-selling book *Jaws.* Charlie was convinced that this great white, attracted by the bloody chum, was simply curious about the boat.

A few others on board didn't want to run either. They had a different idea. "Cap!" one of the men shouted. "Get the harpoon. I want those jaws!" When Charlie refused, the man said, "We paid you. You work for us." It was true. The men had chartered Charlie's boat, and it was his job now to give them what they wanted.

Still he refused. He was remembering another charter boat and another fishing trip, twenty years earlier. Then he was twelve, and his father had taken him deep-sea fishing for the first time. The bluefish were striking. But so were the sharks. Before the fishers could reel in their catches, the sharks were devouring all but the heads of the blues on the lines. Eager to please their paying customers, the charter crew used hooked gaffs and fillet knives tied to the ends of long poles to drive away the scavengers. They stabbed the sharks in the head and in the eyes. Even wounded and bleeding, the sharks continued to feed.

The memory of that wasteful violence had never left Charlie. Now as captain of his own charter boat, he wasn't about to let anyone kill a great white just to make a trophy of its jaws. "If you kill this fish now," Charlie told the men on board the *Snappa*, "the hunt is over. But if you tag it, we may hear about this shark four, five, even eight years from now. It'll be like catching it all over again."

A tagged shark belongs to science. The National Marine Fisheries Service asks anyone who captures a tagged shark to record the fish's length, sex, and condition, then to release it into the ocean again. In that way, scientists can learn about the health and habits of sharks. But the success of tagging programs depends in part on the cooperation of sport and commercial fishers, like Charlie and the others on board.

Still curious, the great white was swimming close to the surface. Charlie put his hand out and touched the shark's head. My shark, he thought. Then he reached for a tagging rod and took aim. When the great white surfaced again, Charlie fired the needle-sharp dart with a plastic tag into the dorsal fin. The shark rolled, violently thrashed the water with its 4-foot (1.2-meter) tail, then dove out of sight.

The men on board the *Snappa* did not see the shark again that day.

It is a fact of life in the ocean that one fish is a meal for another, larger fish. And that fish, in turn, will fill the gullet of another. At the top of this feeding pyramid is the shark. But even the shark is hunted—by humans.

One week after Charlie Donilon had tagged the great white off Block Island, two men fishing in the same area hooked a very large fish. For five hours, they struggled to hold it on the line. Finally, with aching shoulders and cramped hands, the men were able to reel the great fish close to the boat. It was a 16.5-foot (5-meter) great white shark. They harpooned, then shot the fish through the brain. The hunt over, they headed for port. Hours later, they towed the carcass ashore at Mystic, Connecticut.

At 2,800 pounds (1,270 kilograms), the great white was one of the largest sharks ever caught off the east coast of the United States. An excited crowd gathered. Reporters photographed the shark and interviewed the two fishermen. They did not kill the shark to sell its meat, they said. They had landed the shark for sport, for the thrill of defeating a monster. In the days that followed, the men were offered up to $20,000 for the carcass. Instead, they donated it to a science museum.

Was this the same shark that Charlie Donilon had tagged and set free a week earlier? Scientists who had examined the great white did not find a research tag on its dorsal fin. Even so, Charlie believed it was his shark, and it saddened him that such a beautiful wild animal had been killed.

Perhaps one day Charlie will be proven wrong. Maybe another fisher will hook a great white, see the tag that Charlie had pinned onto its dorsal fin in July of 1983, and report the find to the National Marine Fisheries. Then Charlie will know that his shark is still out there somewhere, alive.

THE SHARK TOOK MY LEG!

Chapter Fourteen

The Scream

from Blue Meridian
by Peter Matthiessen

"Have you ever heard a man scream? I mean really scream?" asks Al Giddings. Al has. It is a terrifying sound that Al is not likely to forget for a long time. He heard it one foggy February day in 1963 while scuba diving with friends off the rocky coast of the Farallon Islands, 30 miles (48 kilometers) west of San Francisco.

AL GIDDINGS AND HIS FRIEND LEROY FRENCH had led a group of fifteen divers to the Farallons for a day of spearfishing and photography. The visibility on the bottom, 60 feet [18 meters] down, was poor. Most of the divers, including Al, had already returned to the boat when Leroy came to the surface. Just ahead of him another diver was towing a string of lingcod and rockfish. Fish blood was in the water. Even at the surface, the water roiled and was turbid, with visibility less than 20 feet [6 meters].

Suddenly, Al heard an incredible scream. The sound was so wild that Al couldn't tell that it was Leroy who was screaming for help. Al thought that one of the divers was in trouble with his equipment and had panicked. Al handed his camera to another person on deck and dove into the water, heading for the noise.

Swimming hard, Al lifted his head to get a breath. Thirty feet [9 meters] away, Leroy was screaming at him. "My legs are gone! Help me, Al, don't leave me!" At that moment, an immense fin rose out of the water, wavering silently behind Leroy's head. The two friends were looking right into each other's eyes, and Leroy knew something awful was about to happen. It was the tail fin of a great white shark, and it was about to renew its attack. Leroy saw the shock on Al's face. He heard the heavy thrash in the sea behind him. He gazed hopelessly at his friend. A moment later, he was dragged beneath the surface, and the sea was still.

Al swam to the spot. He felt numb, as if he were swimming in a strange kind of dream. Then Leroy popped up again, not 5 feet [1.5 meters] away. He was hysterical, flailing wildly with both arms and crying out in a high moan. To avoid his clutch, Al swam around behind him and grabbed him by the manifold that connected his twin tanks. The water was cloudly with blood. Dragging Leroy, Al set out on the long slow swim back to the boat.

Meanwhile, the other divers had fled the water, but as Al approached the boat, two men jumped in to help. While Leroy was being eased into the cockpit and the other clambered after him, Al remained dangling from the foot of the ladder. "I tried to stay cool and direct what was going on, but Leroy's blood was cascading down all over the place, and I guess I was there at least two minutes waiting for that shark to return."

Later, Leroy said that his worst moment came when he saw the horror in Al's eyes. On its first attack the shark had enclosed Leroy's buttock, calf, and hand in a bite that must have been 2 feet [60 centimeters] across; the second time it seized him by the foot and ankle. Dragged below the surface, Leroy jabbed the shark furiously with his spear gun, and also released a cartridge in his life vest, which he was wearing that day for the first time in his life. The shark let go. Leroy's wounds required 500 stitches, and he spent four months in the hospital.

Four months after the attack on Leroy, Al warned a group of divers to avoid the Farallons, where incoming ships often dumped their garbage before entering the bay. The men disregarded his advice, and that same afternoon Al heard on the radio that one of the group, Jack Rochette, had been attacked by a great white shark. People in his boat had seen the fin just before Rochette surfaced nearby. Veering, the shark struck him so hard that he was lifted straight out of the water to the level of his waist. But the shark withdrew when Rochette's friends leapt in to help him, and Rochette survived.

Chapter Fifteen

The Eye of the Shark

As a kid, Paul Atkins *loved to listen* to shark stories. He even dreamed of killing a great white. The way he saw it, sharks killed people and that made it all right to kill sharks. It wasn't until he was a teenager diving in the Gulf of Mexico that he saw his first shark in the wild. She was a bull shark, graceful and beautiful. The fact that she could seriously hurt him only made the encounter more exciting. From that first underwater meeting, Paul's attitude about killing wild animals began to change.

Years later, Paul and his wife Grace turned their love of wild animals into a career as wildlife researchers and filmmakers. In 1991, their hunt for the great white shark, the last of the great predators to roam freely on the planet, took them into the waters off the tip of South Africa.

BELOW THE TURBULENT WATERS of the Indian Ocean, it was calm and quiet. Paul Atkins stood in a floating cage made of chicken wire. If a shark charged the wire, the lightweight cage would simply bounce out of the shark's way. Paul searched the shadows below. The great whites were down there, he knew, patrolling the ocean bottom. Their gray backs made it impossible for him to see them. All he could do was wait and hope that they would come to him.

He had no weapon, only a camera. Suddenly, a huge shark rose swiftly, directly toward the cage. As the shark climbed, Paul braced himself against the chicken wire. "Yep! That's you. I've seen pictures of you. This is just what you look like."

The great white circled Paul's cage, then hovered above the top opening. Would the shark attack? And if it did, would the chicken wire bend or would it snap under the force of the animal's charge? What happened next completely surprised Paul. The shark rolled sideways, close to the cage, and stared at him.

Paul looked into its black eye. He remembered a book by Peter Mathiessen. The author had described the eye of a great white shark as "a black hole . . . as empty as the eye of God." But that wasn't what Paul saw. He saw a pupil staring back at him. It was not an empty, soulless eye at all. The realization that he was making contact with a wild, intelligent being electrified Paul. In that moment, looking into the eye of the shark, Paul's attitude about great whites changed forever.

Moments later, the shark vanished into the shadows. In the excitement, Paul had forgotten the camera and missed the shot. But what he had seen he would never forget.

Index